# CAROLS
# FOR LIFE

## VOLUME 1

# COPYRIGHT INFORMATION AND ACKNOWLEDGMENTS

ISBN 08 5402 108 6

Compiled and edited by Leah Perona-Wright and Tim Rogers.
Cover design by Jonathan Bates.
Music origination by the RSCM and Stave Origination.
Printed in Great Britain by Halstan & Co Ltd

RSCM membership is open collectively to churches, colleges and schools, and individually to all interested in church music.

# CONTENTS

# INDEX OF THEMES, FEASTS AND SEASONS

Some of the carols in this collection dwell on a specific Christmas theme while others are suitable for specific seasons and feasts. These are listed below. Carols for general Christmas use are not listed.

Listed with each carol, you will find the item number and the page number.

# PREFACE

*Carols for Life 1* is an exciting new collection which takes a fresh look at Advent, Christmas and Epiphany. Containing over 40 carols, including newly commissioned pieces, *Carols for Life 1* offers fresh and challenging material for the festive season.

Following on in the *Songs for Life* series, *Carols for Life 1* is designed to accompany the RSCM *Voice for Life* training scheme. As with *Songs for Life volumes 1 & 2*, there is an indication of the appropriate *Voice for Life* level. This should enable choir trainers to complement the training scheme with colourful and varied repertoire that singers of all ages and abilities will enjoy.

Canons are particularly useful as preparation for part-singing, encouraging singers to be aware of other parts. Begin by teaching the canon in unison and then, when the melody is secure, gradually build up the number of parts. The canons will also be useful for warm-ups. In addition, the training notes (pages 119-133) suggest sections from some of the songs and canons which may be used as warm-up exercises in rehearsals. The notes also give suggestions for other vocal exercises to develop vocal flexibility, range and strength, enabling singers to deal with the challenges of *Carols for Life 1*.

*Carols for Life 1* also includes sample carol service outlines – one advent carol service and one Christmas service. Contained within each one you will find hymn suggestions and readings as well as suitable carols chosen from the *Carols for Life* collection. When constructing your own carol services you may find it useful to refer to the themes index on p. 4.

*Carols for Life 1* is an indispensable resource that will help church and school choirs celebrate the Christmas season with confidence and style.

# GUIDE TO THE LEVELS

As with *Songs for Life 1*, each song is graded on the contents page according to levels of the *Voice for Life* scheme. This should enable choir trainers to complement the training scheme with new repertoire, and to prepare singers for their *Voice for Life* assessments. The three grades (*Easy*, *Medium* and *Di cult*) are obviously not rigid – what is difficult for one choir may be easier for another – but they are offered as a relative guide to enable you to make the most of the music in this book.

E: *Easy*
| | |
|---|---|
| Children's Voices | Light Blue & Dark Blue level |
| Adult Beginners | Blue level |
| Boys' Changing Voices | Suitable for boys voices who have just changed |

M: *Medium*
| | |
|---|---|
| Children's Voices | Red level |
| Boys' Changing Voices | Level one (suitable for boys with more settled voices) |
| Girls' Developing Voices | Level one |
| Adult Intermediate | Level one |

D: *Difficult*
| | |
|---|---|
| Boys' Changing Voices | Level two (Yellow) |
| Girls' Developing Voices | Level one and two (Yellow) |
| Adult Intermediate | Level two (Yellow) |

\* Where the keyboard part is significantly more demanding than the vocal parts, the grade is marked with an asterisk.

# Behold, I bring you good tidings

Words: Luke 2, 10-11

Music: Antonio Caldara (1670-1736)

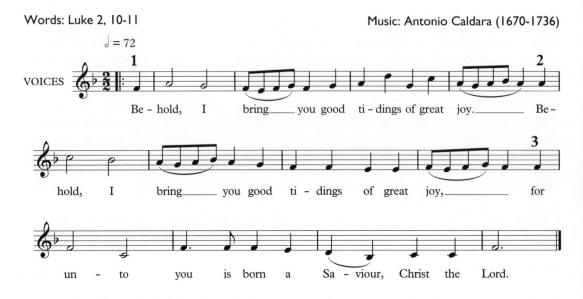

# Christmas is coming

Words & Music: traditional

* Use the alternative text as a prayer refrain

# Gloria!

Words & music: Teresa Brown

# Let's have some more goose

Words: John Fuller

Music: Bryan Kelly

Let's have some more goose and plen-ty of pud-ding! A-noth-er glass of bran-dy! And if we sit quite still, we can't fall ov-er while we sing this song.

This item is also published by RSCM Press as the cover of *A round of carols*

# Lully, lullay

Words: adapted from the Pageant of the
Shearmen and Tailors (15th cent.)

Music: F. J. Haydn (1732-1809)

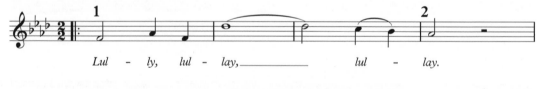

Lul-ly, lul-lay,_____ lul-lay.

O sis-ters too, How may we do, For to pre-serve this day This
He-rod the king, In his rag-ing, Char-ged he hath this day, All
That woe is me, poor child for thee! And ev-er morn and day, For

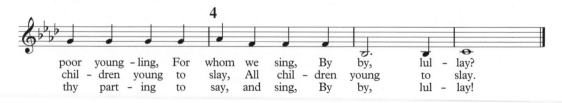

poor young-ling, For whom we sing, By by, lul-lay?
chil-dren young to slay, All chil-dren young to slay.
thy part-ing to say, and sing, By by, lul-lay!

# See Father Christmas

Words & music: traditional

See Fa - ther Christ - mas sit - ting on a stool,

Warm - ing his hands at the blaz - ing yule;

Wrapt in his cloak___ from head to chin, To

keep cold with - out___ and warmth with - in!

# Three kings

Words & Music: Andrew Parnell

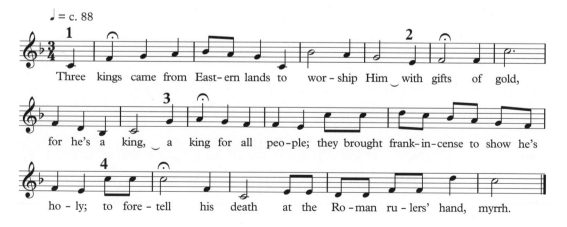

Three kings came from East - ern lands to wor - ship Him with gifts of gold,

for he's a king, a king for all peo - ple; they brought frank - in - cense to show he's

ho - ly; to fore - tell his death at the Ro - man ru - lers' hand, myrrh.

# Tidings in Bethlehem

Words & music: traditional

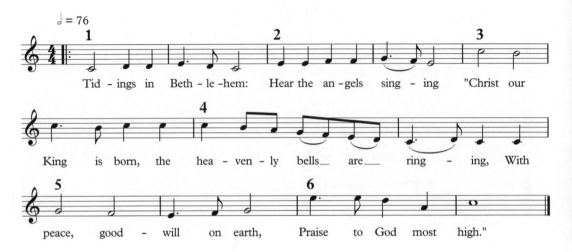

Tid - ings in Beth - le -hem: Hear the an -gels sing - ing "Christ our King is born, the hea - ven - ly bells are ring - ing, With peace, good - will on earth, Praise to God most high."

# 'Tis Christmas time

Words: traditional

Music: William Hayes (1707-77)

'Tis Christ - mas time, the glad - some chime rings out o'er field and fen, Peace, peace, good - will to men, Glad news for all both great and small as Christ - mas comes a - gain.

# Unto us a child is born

Words: Isaiah 9, 6-7

Music: Antonio Caldara (1670-1736)

♩ = 138

1  Un - to us__ a child is born, un - to us__ a son is giv'n,

2  and his name shall_ be call'd, shall_ be call'ed the Prince of Peace.

3  Won - der - ful, Coun - sel - lor, Fa - ther, Prince of Peace.

# Es ist ein' Ros'
## *I know a flower*

Words: traditional fifteenth-century,
English translation by G. R. Woodward

Music: Melchior Vulplus (c.1560-1615)

1  Es is ein' Ros'_____ ent - sprun - gen, Aus ei - ner
   *I know a flow'r_____ it spring - eth, From earth a*

3  Wur - - - - zel zart, Als un die Al - ten sun -
   *ten - - - - der shoot, As old - en pro - phet sing -*

4  - - - gen, Aus Jes - se kam_____ die Art.
   *- - - eth, From Jes - se came_____ the root.*

# A tender shoot

Words: translated by
William Bartholemew (1793-1867)

Music: David Goode

SOPRANO 1

1 A ten - der shoot hath start - ed up from a
2 This shoot, I - sai - ah taught, from Jes - se's

SOPRANO 2
ALTO

A ten - der shoot hath start - ed up from a
2 This shoot, I - sai - ah taught, from Jes - se's

CELLO
(or organ)

*p* *with a certain freedom*

root of grace, as an - cient seers im -
root should spring. The Vir - gin Ma - ry

root of grace, as an - cient seers im -
root should spring. The Vir - gin Ma - ry

part - ed from Jes - se's ho - ly race. It
brought us the branch of which we sing. Our

part - ed from Jes - se's ho - ly race. It
brought us the branch of which we sing. Our

*for Tricia Elcombe*

# Adam lay ybounden

Words: Anonymous, Fifteenth Century

Music: John Turner

Stockport, November 3rd 2000

# Angels, shepherds, people all

Words: David Patrick

Music: Traditional Polish arranged by David Patrick

1.An - gels, shep - herds, peo - ple all tell a - loud the sto - ry
2.Ma - ry, Jo - seph, Je - sus Child in a hum - ble sta - ble,

praise him. O'er the birth-place on that night shone a star so

praise him. O'er the birth-place on that night shone a star so

clear - ly, guid-ing pil-grims to our Sa-viour, loved by all_ so_

clear - ly, guid-ing pil-grims to our Sa-viour, loved by all so

dear - ly.

dear - ly.

# Away in a manger

Words: Anon

Music: Tune by W. J. Kirkpatrick (1838-1921)
arranged by John Sanders

*mf* 2 The cattle are lowing, the baby awakes,
But little Lord Jesus no crying he makes.
I love thee Lord Jesus, look down from the sky,
And stay by my cradle till morning is nigh.

*pp* 3 Be near me, Lord Jesus, I ask thee to stay
Close by me for ever, and love me, I pray!
Bless all the dear children in thy tender care,
And fit us for heaven to live with thee there.

*For Ian Hillier and the Choir of St. George's School, Ascot.*

# Carol of the Advent

Words: Eleanor Farjeon

Music: John Sanders

# Child in the manger

Words: Mary Macdonald (1789-1872)
translated by I. MacBean (1853-1931)

Music: David Sanger

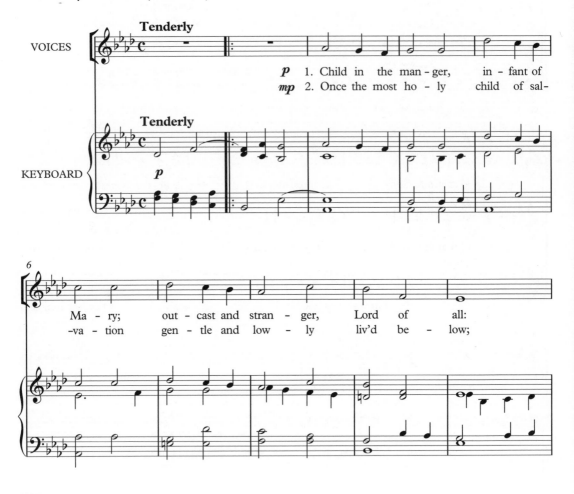

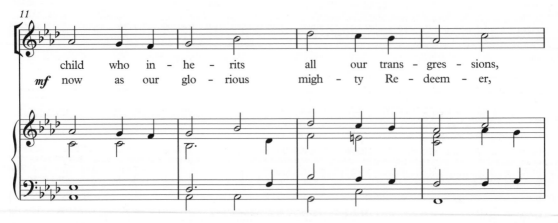

# Gold for a manger bed

Words: Timothy Dudley-Smith

Music: William Llewellyn

the stars___ are shin - ing.
___ so dear - ly bought us.

3.Gold for a mon - arch's state, all things sus-
3.Gold for a mon - arch's state, all things sus-
3.Gold for a mon - arch's state, all things sus - tain - ing;

-tain - ing; high Prince and Po - ten - tate,_ death's dread dis-
- tain - ing; high Prince and Po - ten - tate,_ death's dread dis-
high prince and Po - ten - tate,_ death's dread dis - dain - ing;

# Gaudete!

Words & music: Piae Cantiones, 1582
arranged by Timothy Rogers

*for Honor Sheppard*

# Gloria carol

Words: Anonymous, Fifteenth Century

Music: John Turner

**Very brisk and with great energy**

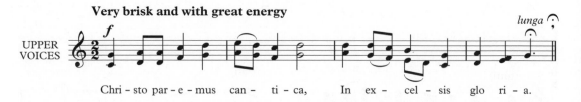

Chri - sto par - e - mus can - ti - ca, In ex - cel - sis glo ri - a.

When Christ was born of Mar - y free, In Beth - lem in that fair_ ci - ty,

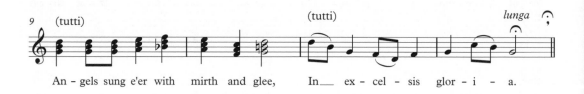

An - gels sung e'er with mirth and glee, In__ ex - cel - sis glor - i - a.

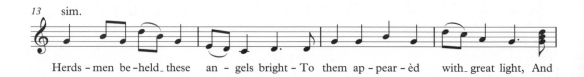

Herds - men be - held_ these an - gels bright - To them ap - pear - èd with_ great light, And

said "God's son is born this night": In__ ex - cel - sis glo - ri - a.

(solo)
*ff*
This king is come to save his kind. In the scrip - ture as we find;

(tutti) (tutti) *lunga*
There - fore this song have we in mind: In ex - cel - sis glo - ri - a.

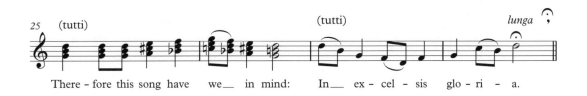

(tutti)
*mf*
Then, dear Lord, for thy great grace, Grant us the bliss to see thy face,

**poco rit.**
(attacca)
Where we may sing to thy sol - ace: In ex - cel - sis glo - ri - a.

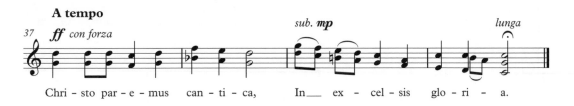

**A tempo**
*ff con forza*          *sub. mp*          *lunga*
Chri - sto par - e - mus can - ti - ca, In ex - cel - sis glo - ri - a.

Stockport, November 3rd 2001

# Hark! a messenger is calling

Words: from the Latin
translated by E. Caswell (1814-78)

Music: Bryan Kelly

So when__ next he comes in glo - ry, And earth's__ fi - nal hour draws near,

So when__ next he comes in glo - ry, And earth's__ fi - nal hour draws near,

May he then as our de - fen - der On the clouds of heaven ap - pear.

May he then as our de - fen - der On the clouds of heaven ap - pear.

Hon - our,__ glo - ry, vir - tue, me - rit, To the__ Fa - ther and the Son,

With the co - e - ter - nal Spi - rit, While un - end - ing a - ges run.

# He comes, the Way that all may tread

Words: Timothy Dudley-Smith

Music: William Llewellyn

1. He comes, the Way that all may tread, the Shep - herd King of Da-vid's line, the ra - diance from his man - ger bed through all the earth shall shine: Al - le - lu - ia, Al - le - lu - ia,

2. He comes, the Truth the pro-phets heard, who was and is and is to be, God's time-less, true e - ter - nal Word, whom wise men longed to see:

# I sing of a maiden

Words: anonymous
15th century English carol

Music: Louis Halsey

**Gently flowing, tenderly** ♩ = c.92

VOICES

I
*p*

I sing___ of a mai - den that is

**Gently flowing, tenderly** ♩ = c.92

KEYBOARD

*p*

*p*

5

ma - ke - less;___ King___ of all kings To her son she ches.

*cresc.*

II
*p*

He

*cresc.*

*p*

10

came___ all so still___ There his mo - ther was, As dew___ in

*cresc.*

*cresc.*

# It came upon the midnight clear

Words: Edmund Hamilton Sears (1810-76)

Music: Richard Storrs Willis (1819-1900)
arranged by Philip Ledger

world in so - lemn still - ness lay To hear the an - gels sing.
hush the noise, ye men of strife, And hear the an - gels sing.

2. Still
4. For

2. Through clo - ven skies they come, With wings un - furled;_
4. The days_ are haste - ning on, By bards fore - told,_

through the clo - ven skies they come, With peace - ful wings un - furled;_ And
lo! the days_ are haste - ning on, By pro - phet - bards fore - told,_ When,

# Maranatha, alleluia!

Words: John Brownlie (1857-1925)

Music: David Ogden

An alternative arrangement for SAMen is also published by RSCM Press in *Songs for Life, volume 2.*

50

# Over distant land afar

Words: David Patrick

Music: Folk Melody from the Philippines
arranged by David Patrick

# Noël let us sing

Words: translated by Philip Ledger

Music: traditional French carol
arranged by Philip Ledger

*For Paul Dewhurst and Thomas's London Day School Choir*

# Nova, nova

Words: Annunciation carol,
15th century

Music: Alan Spedding

\* News! News! 'Ave' is made from 'Eva' (i.e. Virgin Mary is the new Eve)

62

# O my dear heart

Words: James, John
and Robert Wedderburn

Music: Peter Aston

# Quem pastores laudavere

Ronald Corp

glo – ri – a!'

glo – ri – a!'

# Still, still, still

Words: German carol with
English translation by Louis Halsey

Music: German carol
arranged by Louis Halsey

# Ring out with jocund chime

Words: John Rishton Jackson (d. 1924)

Music: Colin Hand

76

# Sweet baby sleep!

Words: George Wither (1588-1667)

Music: Bryan Kelly

S.1
1. My__ pret-ty lamb,__ for-bear to weep; Be__ still my dear; sweet ba-by sleep.
2. Sweet__ ba-by, then__ for-bear to weep; Be__ still my dear; sweet ba-by sleep.

S.2
A.
mm_____

S.1 & S.2
The King__ of Kings,__ when he__ was born, Had

A.
The King__ of Kings, when he__ was

not__ so much__ for out-ward ease; By him__ such dress - ings

born, Had not so much for out - ward ease;__ By him__ such dress - ings

were___ not worn, Nor such___ like swad - dling clothes as these.

were___ not worn, Nor such___ like swad - dling clothes as these.

Sweet ba - by, then,___ for - bear to weep; Be___ still, my babe; sweet ba - by, sleep.

mm_____

The wants that he___ did then___ sus - tain Have

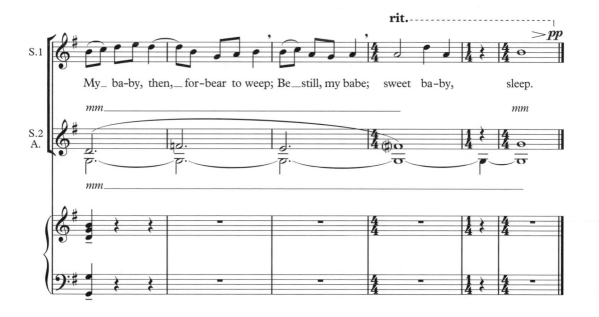

*For many altos...*

# The darkest midnight in December

Music: traditional Irish carol
arranged by Andrew Johnstone

glo - rious charms;___ Born___ of a___ maid,___ as
from all harms;___ Then___ let us___ sing___ and

pro - phets___ said,___ The_ God of___ Love___ in
wel - come___ him,___ The_ God of___ Love___ in

Ma - ry's arms.___
Ma - ry's arms.___

rall.

*For the choir of Queen Margaret's School, York*

# Unfinished story

Words & music by Philip Godfrey

It was a night in De-cem-ber, cold De-cem-ber when a light came into our world; a light sent from up a-bove us one night Beth-le-hem be-held. But is that night in De-cem-ber all we re-mem-ber of the

way a-head. But will the world e-ver hear him, ga - ther near him as a

said. But will the world e-ver hear him, ga - ther near him as a

guide, guar-di-an and friend? An un - fin-ished sto - ry___ is

guide, guar-di-an and friend? An un - fin-ished sto - ry___

what we are hear-ing,___ Re - joice!___

but we can de-ter- mine its end. all the an-

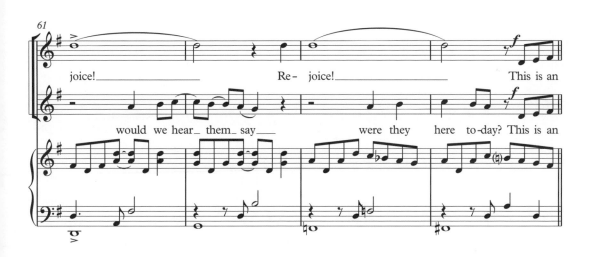

un-fin-ished sto-ry, filled with glo-ry such as we can-not com-pre-hend. A

un-fin-ished sto-ry, filled with glo-ry such as we can-not com-pre-hend. A

won - der - ful sto - ry,_ and we have been gi - ven_ the chance to com-plete_ it, a

won - der - ful sto - ry,_

chance that we must_ not sus - pend;_

the chance to com- plete_ it _ the

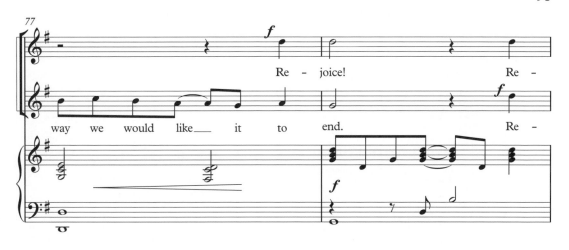

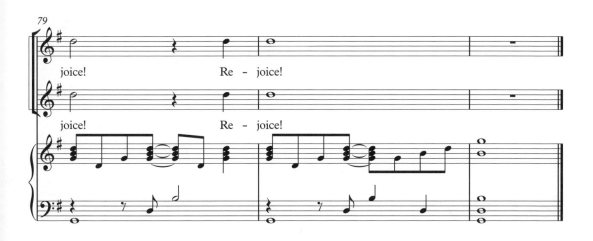

# The joyful sounds of salvation

Words: from Husk's
*Songs of the Nativity* (1855)

Music: English traditional melody
arranged by Philip Ledger

To - ge - ther__ did pass;
In fields that__ did lie,
Ap - peared in__ the sky,

Jo - seph and__ Ma - ry to - ge - ther did pass; These
cer - tain poor__ shep - herds in__ fields__ that did lie, And
great host of__ an - gels ap - peared in the sky, Who

That Jo - seph and__ Ma - ry__ did pass;
To shep - herds in__ fields that__ did lie,
A great host ap - peared in__ the sky,

The o - thers did go,
No long - er to stay,
And sweet - ly did sing;

two to__ be tax'd with__ the__ o - thers did go, For__
bade them__ no long - er__ in__ sor - row to stay, For__
mer - ri - ly talk - ed,__ and__ sweet - ly did sing; All__

These two with the__ o - thers did go,
And bade them no__ long - er to stay,
Who talk - ed, and__ sweet - ly did sing;

Com - mand - ed__ it so.
Was born on__ that day.
To God and__ their king.

Cae - sar__ com - mand - ed__ and__ or - dered it so.
their_ bless - ed__ Sav - iour was__ born on that day.
glo - ry__ to__ God and__ their_ hea - ven - ly king.

For__ Cae - sar__ com - mand - ed__ it so.
Their Sav - iour_ was__ born on__ that day.
All__ glo - ry__ to__ God and__ their king.

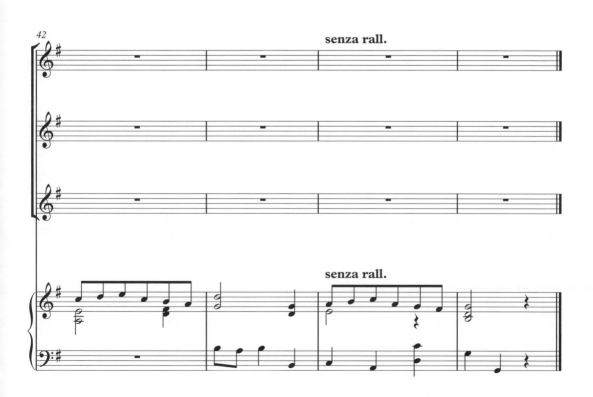

senza rall.

senza rall.

*For M.I.F. with love*

# The rose-tree carol

Words: Peter Winckworth,
from *Christmas Cards*, published by
The Church Literature Association in 1962

Music: Barry Ferguson

2. A rose-tree grew at Bethlehem, On which so piercing thorns did grow; A shepherd's fingers twined, twined its stem To make a crown for Jesu's brow. Red rose, red rose, Blood red, I cry; Red rose, red rose, Red for Calvary, Red rose, red rose, Red for Calvary.

A shepherd twined, twined its stem To make a

Rochester 20 October 1986

# Waiting for the word

Words & music: Peter Skellern

This work is also published by RSCM Press in a version for mixed voices and keyboard.

waiting___ for the word.___ Let me know you're here, call me loud and clear for as yet I have not heard,___ I could shine a light, I could fight the fight, I'm just waiting___ for the word.__

mp

I would

wait-ing___ for the word.___ Though I'm full of doubt do not turn me out, we are lost who have not heard,_____ I will strive to be what you want of me while I'm wait-ing___ for the word.__ I'm just wait-ing___ for the word._____

# Watts's cradle song

Words: Isaac Watts (1674-1748)          Music: Alan Spedding

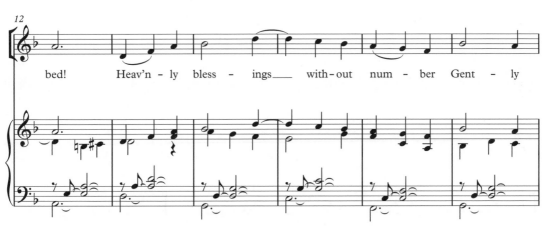

fall - ing on thy head.

2 Sleep my babe; thy food and rai - ment, House and home thy

2 Sleep my babe thy food and rai - ment, House and home thy

friends pro - vide; All with - out thy care and pay - ment,

friends pro - vide; All with - out thy care and pay - ment,

All thy wants are well sup-plied.

3 Soft and ea-sy is thy cra-dle; Coarse and hard thy Sa-viour lay, When his birth - place was a sta-ble And his soft-est bed was

58

hay. Lo,—— he

63

slum - bers in—— his man - ger, Where the horn - èd

68

ox - en fed; Peace,—— my dar - ling!—— here's no

73

dan - ger;—— Here's no ox—— a - near—— thy bed.

# Welcome Yule

Words: anonymous
15th century carol

Music: Colin Hand

112

# What star is this?

Words: C Coffin (1676-1749)
Tr. J Chandler (1806-1876)

Andrew Parnell (b.1954)

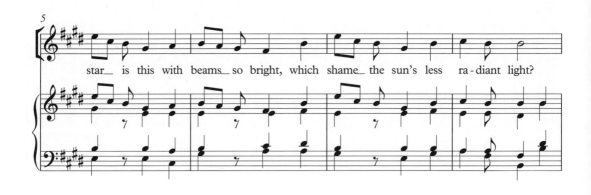

star__ is this with beams__ so bright, which shame__ the sun's less ra-diant light?

'Tis sent to an-nounce a new-born__King, Glad ti-dings of our God to bring.

116

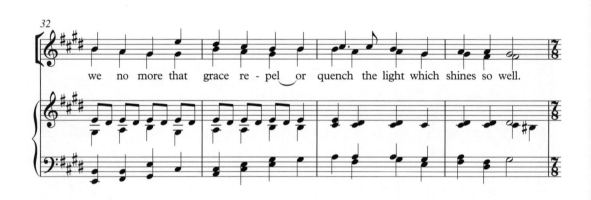

117

# Zither Carol

Words: Malcolm Sargent

Music: Czech folk tune
arranged by John Sanders

2 *mf* Shepherds came at the fame of thy name,
  Angels their guide to Bethlehem.
  In that place saw thy face filled with grace,
  Stood at thy door.
*f* "Hallelujah" etc.
  Love evermore.

3 *mf* Wise men too haste to do homage new,
  Gold, myrrh and frankincense they bring.
  As 'twas said starlight led to thy bed,
*p* Bending their knee.
*f* "Hallelujah" etc.
  Worshipping thee.

4 *f* Cherubim Seraphim worship him,
  Sun, moon and stars proclaim his power.
  Everyday on our way we shall say
*ff* Hallelujah.
*ff* "Hallelujah" etc.
  Hallelujah.

# CAROL SERVICES IN ADVENT AND CHRISTMAS

The carols in this book can be used during regular worship in Advent and Christmas and in special carol services. Two flexible outlines of carol services are included here. They can be adapted easily to suit available resources and the needs of different occasions; the hymns can be found in most hymn books.

Advent is more than just 'a time of preparation for Christmas'. The Church has always used this season to contemplate the various 'comings' of Christ: his coming as a baby in Bethlehem; his coming to the Jewish people, pointed out by John the Baptist; and his coming again in glory to judge the living and dead. The Advent service reflects this richness in words and music. The Christmas service contemplates the baby of Bethlehem, foretold by the prophets, born of the virgin Mary, welcomed by the shepherds and the magi, witnessed to by the gospels.

## AN ADVENT CAROL SERVICE

**GATHERING**

| | |
|---|---|
| Organ or instrumental prelude | |
| All | O come, O come Emmanuel |
| Sentence | Matthew 1: 23 |
| Introduction and welcome | |

**THE WORD**

| | |
|---|---|
| Choir | Adam lay ybounden |
| Reading | Isaiah 9: 2-7 |
| Choir | A tender shoot |
| All | Long ago, prophets knew |
| Reading | Malachi 3: 1-4 |
| Choir | Hark, a messenger is calling |
| Reading | Mark 1: 1-8 |
| All | On Jordan's bank the Baptist's cry |
| Choir | Maranatha, alleluia |
| Reading | Isaiah 7: 10-14 |
| All | Gabriel's message does away |
| Choir | Carol of the Advent |
| Reading | Matthew 1: 18-25 |
| Choir | I sing of a maiden |
| Reading | Luke 1: 26-38 |
| All | The angel Gabriel from heaven came |
| Choir | Nova! Nova! |
| Organ or instrumental interlude, or sermon | |

**PRAYER**

| | |
|---|---|
| Canticle | Magnificat, or Tell out my soul |
| Prayers (with sung response) | Christmas is coming (alternative text) |
| Lord's Prayer and collect | Collect from the Fourth Sunday of Advent |

**SENDING FORTH**

| | |
|---|---|
| Blessing | |
| All | Lo, he comes with clouds descending |

# A CHRISTMAS CAROL SERVICE

**GATHERING**

| | |
|---|---|
| Organ or instrumental prelude | |
| All | Once in royal David's city |
| Sentence | John 1: 14 |
| Introduction and welcome | |

**THE WORD**

| | |
|---|---|
| Choir | Gaudete, or Adam lay ybounden |
| Reading | Isaiah 9: 2-7 |
| All | Unto us is born a son |
| Choir | Ring out with jocund chime |
| Reading | Isaiah 11: 1-4 |
| All | Of the Father's heart begotten |
| Choir | Noël let us sing, or Gold for a manger bed |
| Reading | Luke 1: 26-38 |
| All | The angel Gabriel from heaven came |
| Choir | Nova! Nova! |
| Reading | Luke 2: 1-7 |
| All | Silent night |
| Choir | Away in a manger, or Sweet baby sleep |
| Reading | Luke 2: 8-16 |
| All | While shepherds watched their flocks |
| Choir | Angels, shepherds |
| Reading | Matthew 2: 1-11 (magi) |
| All | As with gladness men of old |
| Choir | Quem pastores laudavere |
| Reading | John 1: 1-14 |
| All | O come all ye faithful |
| Organ or instrumental interlude, or sermon | |

**PRAYER**

| | |
|---|---|
| Canticle | Te Deum |
| Prayers (with sung response) | Christmas is coming (alternative text) |
| Lord's Prayer and collect | Collect for Christmas Day |

**SENDING FORTH**

Blessing

# TRAINING NOTES

**1.  Behold, I bring you good tidings**

- The text of the canon needs to be well articulated in order to achieve a sprightly and exciting performance. Roll your 'r' in words like 'bring' as this will give a good explosive start to the quaver pattern while also brightening up the sound. Make sure consonants such as the 'h' of 'Behold' are audible – this kind of consonant is often neglected but if well articulated can have a magical effect on the music.

- Take care with the diphthong 'Joy'. Keep the vowel open for as long as possible, only altering the sound right at the end (e.g., encourage the choir to sing 'Jaw' for the quaver movement, and add the 'oi' sound on the final crotchet). This will keep the vowel sound pure.

- Sing the quaver movement in bars 2 and 4, emphasizing the first quaver in each group only. This will make the quaver pattern easier to sing and make the phrase sound effortless. Use the following exercise to practise this technique:

- Take care in the third complete bar to be accurate with both of the upward leaps of a fourth, as well as the downward fifths. These must be seamless. Practise this exercise, if necessary:

- You will find alternative words for this canon in *Songs for life 2*.

**2.  Christmas is coming**

- This canon needs crisp articulation of the text. Ensure that the 't' of 'Christmas' is audible, and take particular care over the quaver pattern ('and the', in bar 10). Because of the tempo there is a danger that the 'd' of 'and' will not sound. You will really need to work your tongue hard here! You could try warming up your choir with a tongue twister at the start of the practice in order to get their tongues, teeth, and lips moving.

- Although the text must be well articulated, and the tempo is fast, the canon should not be sung entirely staccato or with the first beat of every bar accented as this will become tedious. Keep the repeated notes at the beginning of lines 1 and 2 legato and aim towards the last of the group e.g., 'Christmas is <u>com</u>ing' and 'Cold is the <u>night</u>'. A small emphasis on these words will provide a sense of progression through the repeated notes, and will help to keep the dotted rhythms that follow as bouncy as possible, while also making sense of the words.

- Try phrasing off at the end of each four bar phrase to prevent the final bar of each line being too heavily accented, and so that each line is a complete phrase in itself.

- Using the alternative text, this piece can be used as a sung response to intercessions, sung through once each time in unison.

### 3. Gloria

*Glory to God in the highest*

- Sing this rhythmically, joyfully and with a smile.
- The careful articulation of syncopated rhythms is important in order to achieve an exciting performance of the 'Gloria!'
- Always lighten the last syllable of the word Gloria. In Section 2, be prepared for the quaver rests. Thinking in quavers during the minims may be helpful here. In Section 3, practise bar 4 on its own until the rhythm is secure, using the following exercise.

De - o, De - o,De-o    De - o, De - o,De-o    De - o, De - o,De-o    De - o, De - o,De-o

Aim to keep the placing of the voice the same at each octave and sing four bars in one breath, from 'in excelsis Deo' to the end of the next 'Gloria'. When you return to the original music the octave leap should sound effortless.

- Once all the parts are underway, enjoy the sound, remember: it's about angels bringing good news.

### 4. Let's have some more goose

- Take care over the rhythms – practise them either by clapping the rhythm through first, or by saying the text in rhythm before you add the notes and the articulation.
- Take some time to look at all the articulation marks (staccato, accents, and tenuto) and decide exactly how each should be performed. Do not give each of the articulation marks the same emphasis, as this will only slow the tempo and produce a rather laboured performance. Remember that tenuto (meaning 'held on') is not the same as an accent. Having practised saying the words in rhythm, try repeating this exercise focusing on the articulation to make it as varied and exciting as possible.
- Be aware of the difference between the rising quaver figures 'Let's have some' and 'And if we sit'. The first of these phrases rises up the third immediately, while the latter phrase repeats the first note before rising up the scale.
- There is no time at the end of the canon to pause if you intend to repeat it from the beginning again. However, the phrases are short so you may find that you do not need to breathe at the end, and can run the final phrase straight into the first phrase. If you do need to breathe, it must be quick!
- Above all things, remember to aim for a light and lively performance.

### 5. Lully, lullay

- Keep this canon as legato and fluid as possible.
  The first phrase will need practice in order to tune each interval carefully and to ensure a smooth transition between the two notes of the minor sixth interval.
- On the few long notes in the canon, do not keep the volume constant – add your own dynamics to give as much musical shape as you can.
- With the repeated crotchets (at the start of the second line), try to keep the phrase legato, emphasize only the important words in the text, and try not to breathe at every comma; this will give a sense of forward movement and fluidity.
- The beginning of the second line is high in the voice and needs to be supported well. By the same token the lowest notes at the end of the canon must not be neglected.
- Take care over repeated notes that they do not flatten in pitch.
- Ensure that the raised seventh (the E natural) is kept bright and well-tuned.

6. **See Father Christmas**
- This canon can be used to perfect the tuning of semitones and to help singers differentiate accurately between semitones and tones.
- Ensure that the G natural in bar 5 is kept bright – after singing A flat earlier in the bar there is a danger that the G will sound slightly flat.
- In bar 2, try to give a little extra emphasis to the B flat. As the lowest note in a fast moving phrase, this may be missed if it is not well supported.
- Descending semitone movement has a tendency to flatten in pitch. Remember how close together the intervals are, and keep the sound bright.
- Remember to articulate the words well. This canon can be made to sound humorous if the words are audible and emphasized correctly, and if the semitone movement is brought out.

7. **Three kings**
- The melodic line of this round is largely scalic, but some of the intervals are a little awkward. The singers will need to be confident in pitching these, especially when they are singing 'against' the other voices. These passages (e.g., 'gold, for he's a King'; '-tell his death' and 'rulers' hand, myrrh') could be isolated and made into small exercises.
- As in a seventeenth-century catch, when all four voices are singing, a phrase of words shared by three parts should project from the general texture. In order to achieve this, the following words need to be given special prominence: 'of gold', 'frankincense', '(h)and myrrh' and '-tell'.
- Good breath control will be needed particularly for the first and second phrases. Try to observe the slurs and breath marks – this will add to the forward momentum of the round.
- Decide whether to finish with all four parts singing (at the pause sign and on the key-chord) or with one part, for which there are various possibilities, so long as good sense in the words is maintained. The best places are probably 'worship him', 'with gifts', 'he's a king' or 'all people'.

8. **Tidings in Bethlehem**
- This canon is a proclamation of the birth of Christ. In order to create an impression of a majestic fanfare, keep the dotted rhythms strict and give them a little extra emphasis.
- Take care not to rush the descending scale of quavers.
- Make the most of the words. In particular, try to roll your 'r's – especially on the word 'ringing'.

9. **'Tis Christmas time**
- Try to keep in mind the sound of ringing church bells while singing this canon. This will help you to produce a joyful and vital performance. Try not to sing too legato, but rather aim for a light tone and well-articulated words.
- Keep the dotted rhythms lively.
- Take care not to over emphasize the top E flat in the first line – there will be a tendency to accent this note because it is high in the voice. However, the words demand a far more gentle approach to this note so that the emphasis falls on the beginning of the next bar: 'the glad̲some'.
- Count carefully on the longer notes to ensure that the 'c' of 'peace' is placed exactly on the rest.

10. **Unto us a child is born**
- Bars 5-8 are less important than bars 1-4. The dynamic level should reflect the fact that the material accompanies the melody of the opening section.
- Experiment with the effects of singing bars 1-4 in two bar phrases and in one phrase. Then make a choice to suit your choir and the building where your performance will take place.
- The entries in bars 9-11 should be rhythmically precise – neither early nor late.

### 11. Es ist ein' Ros'

- This canon needs to be sung legato, but with due care and emphasis on the syncopated rhythms in bars 8-9 and the dotted rhythms in bars 2 and 11.
- Make the most of each musical phrase by accenting the important words (e.g., Es ist ein' <u>Ros'</u> ent<u>sprung</u>en), and ensure that each phrase is not finished with a heavily accented note. The final note in each phrase needs to be carefully placed (not 'snatched') but phrased-off (sung with less volume than the previous note). Although this is difficult to achieve when trying to take a breath before the next phrase, try to keep the joining of phrases as relaxed as possible.
- Be aware that repeated notes have a tendency to flatten in pitch. To counteract this in the first bar, aim towards the E (in bar 2) as the high point in the phrase both in pitch and dynamic.
- The falling fourth in bar 2 may need attention in order to tune the interval precisely.

### 12. A tender shoot

- Try to create a mysterious, radiant atmosphere when performing this carol.
- Focus on achieving legato phrases and long melodic lines, encouraging your singers not to breathe in the middle of phrases. The use of cresendi and diminuendi will help to shape each phrase effectively.
- Although the harmony is quite rich, and some of the modulations may appear daunting at first sight, each part is simple enough when sung on its own – often moving by step. Practise each part independently and without the cello/organ accompaniment. Once your singers are confident of their own parts then you can put all the parts together with the accompaniment.
- Practise the tuning of the modulation in bars 9-10 unaccompanied so that the semitone movement becomes natural for your singers. Then add the cello/organ part – there is a semitone dissonance here between the vocal parts and the accompaniment, so the singers need to be confident about their part.
- In particular the modulations in bars 12-14 will be difficult to tune. Encourage your singers to concentrate on the difference between tone and semitone movement here and to ensure that the falling semitones do not flatten in pitch.

### 13. Adam Lay ybounden

- The four verses of this carol progress from gloom to exultation, and each verse has a more consonant harmony than the previous one, culminating in a radiant D Major.
- The dynamics emphasize the change in mood which takes place in both the text and the music. For an effective and exciting performance, make sure these are brought out.
- The vocal line, though very straightforward in itself, needs to be sung legato and with careful attention to the tuning (so that the expressive clashes with the accompaniment sound both deliberate and natural).
- Bars 35-38 will need practice to achieve an effortless leap from the low E up a ninth to the F sharp. You may also need to draw your singers' attention to the difference between the falling phrases here in bars 35 and 37.
- The accompaniment can be played on either harp or piano – the small subsidiary bass notes can be omitted if desired.

### 14. Angels, shepherds, people all

- This traditional Polish melody should be sung in a bright, rhythmic and buoyant way.
- Enjoy the key change at bar 33 and be sure that the accompanist brings out the melody in bars 41-48.
- Try to achieve the feeling of 4-bar phrases (rather than 2-bar phrases) and adjust your breathing accordingly.

- Note the dynamic difference between verses 1 and 2 and the word underlay in the alto part in bars 6, 12 and 40.
- Ensure that sopranos and altos support the sound properly – particularly during the descant, so that they get right to the heart of the upper notes here.
- Try and bring out the sequence between the staggered entries in bars 13 and 14, and bars 17 and 18.
- Practise the tuning of the rising sixth figure in bar 15.
- Clearly projected diction is essential. Remember that you are telling a story (however well-known it may be)!

## 15. Away in a manger
- This is essentially a lullaby and needs to be performed in a smooth and simple style. As a general rule, try to sing and breathe in four-bar phrases. The exception is in verse 3 when you need to breathe after 'Jesus' in line 1 and carry on to the word 'ever' in line 2.
- This would make a good exercise for improving vowel sounds. Try singing each verse *molto legato* omitting the consonants and using only the vowels.
- Variety could be attained using the following scheme. Verse 1: solo voice only singing the tune. Verse 2: solo voice, semi-chorus or all first sopranos singing the soprano 1 part while soprano 2 and altos hum. Verse 3: all voices sing normally.
- Note that the last 3 notes of the tune are in the soprano 2 part and should not be overwhelmed by soprano 1.

## 16. Carol of the Advent
- Bearing in mind the meaning of the words, sing this carol with energy and excitement.
- The music could be used as an exercise in intonation. The G natural in bars 6 and 7 in soprano 2 will need careful tuning especially when it becomes G sharp again in bar 10. The change of key in verse 2, bars 20-32, is difficult to manage and slow practice is recommended particularly when it returns to the major mode at 'People look East' in bar 32.
- The final bar of each verse ends with a G natural in the alto followed immediately by a G sharp in soprano 2, – ensure that these are accurate.
- Athletic manipulation of the lips, teeth and tongue are needed to achieve crisp diction.
- Breath marks are provided but in each verse bars 13 and 14 should carry on without a break.
- The crescendi and diminuendi should be carefully graded to make their full effect on the text and also to create variety among the 4 verses.

## 17. Child in a manger
- Try to sing this with tenderness, as a lullaby.
- Decide on your breathing before singing the piece through. If you decide to breathe at each of the punctuation marks in the first 10 bars, keep these breaths as small as possible so that they do not interfere with the flow of the melody.
- Make sure bars 11-14 are sung in one breath and likewise bars 15-18.
- Many of the phrases in the descant begin and end in unison with the melody – make sure both parts listen to each other and tune these notes carefully.
- Bar 32 will need careful tuning as the descant and melody are a major seventh apart. Practise each part separately and then put them together.
- Make sure the singers of the descant remember their crotchet rest in bar 33 – this is the only time a phrase begins off the beat and it is a catch.

### 18. Gold for a Manger Bed

- The opening verses describe Jesus in the manger and need to be sung with tenderness. Keep the melody and accompaniment flowing gently so that the syncopations do not sound jerky – imagine you are singing a lullaby and that you are rocking the cradle gently.
- By verse 3 the text has moved on to the realization that Jesus is not only a baby, but also a heavenly King and Saviour. To emphasize this change in the text and to attain variety you could try the following scheme: verse 1: solo, verse 2: semi-chorus or all voices in unison, verse 3: full harmony.
- During verse 3, all the parts need to be loud and energetic, but make sure that the tune is audible – remember that the melody is in the alto part at this point.
- The syncopated rhythms will need practice to ensure that they are tidy. In particular, bars 32-39 will need attention as all the parts are moving together. Try speaking the text in rhythm first before adding the notes.
- Remember to bring the dynamic right back to *pp* for the last phrase in order to communicate the intimacy and vulnerability of Jesus, the new born baby, in the manger.

### 19. Gaudete!

*Refrain: Rejoice! Rejoice! Christ is born of the Virgin Mary; rejoice!*

1. *The time of grace is now here for which we have prayed;*
   *songs of joy let us devoutly render.*
2. *God is made man, to the astonishment of nature;*
   *The world is renewed by Christ reigning.*
3. *The gate of Ezekiel, once closed, has been passed through;*
   *From whence light has risen, salvation is found.*
4. *Therefore let our gathering sing praises now at this time of purification;*
   *Let it bless the Lord: hail our King.*

- The unusual canonic treatment of the verses creates dissonance. Each line should move forwards; don't let the music be dragged back by the notation of crotchets. Exaggerate the question and answer elements in the phrases.
- Good ensemble is required as singers must be aware of the points when their own phrase needs to be heard above the other and vice versa. Crescendo then diminuendo.
- During the refrain, emphasize the cross-rhythms as much as possible without slowing the tempo
- Make sure the octave intervals between alto and soprano 1 are tuned carefully in the refrain.
- At the end of the refrain keep the B natural in soprano 1 as bright as possible.

### 20. Gloria Carol

*Refrain: Let us set forth songs to Christ, glory in the highest.*

- A certain roughness is appropriate in singing this medieval-sounding carol – try to sing without vibrato.
- The melody should be sung strictly in time and very rhythmically. The pauses at the end of the verses can be long, but make sure that this does not slow the speed of the piece. This carol needs to be full of vigour and requires a sustained momentum throughout.
- As the piece is unaccompanied, try to fix the tonic in your mind – the majority of phrases start and end on the tonic note (G) and you need to make sure both parts come back to the same pitch to keep the tuning good.
- The opening and closing passages, with their organum-like parallel fifths and fourths, should be sung forcefully – almost nasally. However, take care over the tuning here: remember that loud singing has a tendency to sharpen in pitch and make sure both parts come back to exactly the same

d of the line.

e constantly changes between unison, 2-part and 3-part writing. Make sure that the
ns are as equal as possible.

the dynamic strong throughout the piece – the quietest dynamic is *mf* and the loudest is *ff*.

y in the last two bars should the dynamic drop to *mp* in order to crescendo back to *ff* – this will
vide a dramatic and effective conclusion to your performance.

### Hark! a messenger is calling

Most of this setting needs robust singing. However, do take note of the dynamic markings to give
the required contrasts.

- Imagine the melody is a trumpet fanfare announcing the triumphant arrival of a king – (the birth of
Christ). Strong accents are wanted to underline the extrovert nature of the music.
- There are only 3 quiet phrases in this piece – make sure these are a real contrast to the loud
sections in order to emphasize the text at these points
- You may need to rehearse soprano 1 separately in bar 16 to practise the E down to the A. Although
this interval is simple when sung on its own, the soprano 1 falls to a dissonance here against
soprano 2 which is tricky.
- Ensure the changes in key are well-tuned and seamless.

### 22. He comes, the Way that all may tread

- This carol should be sung with energy and a feeling of excitement at Christ's coming. In particular,
try to keep the syncopated rhythms as precise and bouncy as possible – this will help to achieve an
exuberant performance.
- Try singing the first phrase to 'Bom, bom', then 'Bin, bin' and finally to a staccato 'Ha! ha!' Then
sing the lyrics with the first phrase, and aim to make them as clear and well articulated as these
initial exercises.
- Although the piece is quite fast, take care that it does not speed up and run away with itself.
- In bar 13 you may like to practise the crescendo to ensure that there is a gradual increase in volume
over the whole bar, rather than a sudden increase in volume at the beginning of bar 14. The
following exercise will help:

- In verse 3 the parts move together rhythmically for the majority of the verse. However, in bars 33-
34 the altos have a different syncopated rhythm to that in the soprano part. Practise these parts
separately before putting them together.
- In bars 25-26 and 33-34 there is some close harmony with soprano 1 and soprano 2 moving in
consecutive 2nds. This will need rehearsing so that each part is confident with its own line and can
listen carefully in order to tune the chords accurately.
- The last bar must be firm, but not shouted. Although the last note needs to be short, don't snatch or
hurry it.

### 23. I sing of a maiden

- This setting of a well-known English medieval carol-text in honour of the Virgin Mary performed with a relaxed serenity, an unhurried flow and a real legato; the quavers in pa would benefit from being sung 'tenuto'.
- Good breath control is necessary in order to sing through the 3- and 4-bar phrases.
- Take special care over the downward leaps of a seventh (bars 4, 6-7, etc.), so that they soun confident. Avoid any obvious change of tone-quality between the upper and lower notes. Lik take special care over the intervals in both parts between bars 21-22 – both parts fall to a sem dissonance – this will be tricky to tune and need work to sound confident.
- The dynamic markings should be helpful in shaping the phrases, and a sensitive 'colouring' of important words will give any performance an extra refinement.

### 24. It came upon the midnight clear

- Sing this carol with legato phrases avoiding any bumps in the rhythm and taking care that the F sharps are not flat.
- The following exercise could help:

- Take care for verses 2 and 4 that the melody, in the lower part, can be heard.
- Keep a lilting 2 in a bar feel.

### 25. Maranatha, alleluia!

- 'Maranatha' is an Aramaic word used by early Christians meaning: *Our Lord, come!*
- The irregular time signature may cause some confusion. Ensure that the melody flows seamlessly though the time changes.
- Each appearance of the refrain 'Maranatha' needs to be majestic in character.
- Ensure that the tempo is not too slow, or the triplets will be more difficult to sing.
- Identify the breathing points carefully so that the meaning of the text is not obscured.
- A three-part version of 'Maranatha, alleluia!' can be found in *Songs for Life 2.*

### 26. Over distant land afar

- This setting of a traditional folk melody from the Philippines needs to be sung in a sustained style with good attention to dynamic markings.
- Bright and crisp consonants are needed throughout.
- At all times be sure to shape the phrases sensitively and build each phrase to its logical climax.
- The 'Sing for joy' chorus needs to contrast in mood with the verse preceding it. Let the music 'smile' here.
- The verses need to be breathed in 2-bar phrases but at all times let the sense of the words dictate where to breathe. Avoid breathing at every comma.
- All parts need to keep the third of the chord (often the G sharp) bright and in tune.
- Soprano 1 needs to take care over the tuning of the rising fourth in bars 5, 17 and 29.
- Really enjoy the last two bars!

### 27. Noël let us sing

- Articulation of the words is particularly important here; practise the exercise below with exaggerated consonants:

- As there are 6 verses, try to provide variety with dynamic difference. You could also allot a solo verse – verse 3 would be particularly well suited to being sung as a solo.
- In the descant, make sure that the raised seventh (D sharp) is as bright as possible each time it comes. In bar 35, make sure you do not make your falling semitone too large or the pitch will flatten - keep the A sharp bright and well-tuned.

### 28. Nova! Nova!

Refrain: *News! News! Ave is made from Eva*
Verse 5: *(Ecce ancilla Domini) Behold the handmaid of the Lord.*

- The text of the refrain draws on wordplay typical in medieval devotional writing: the greeting of the angel Gabriel to Mary ('Ave'), reverses the name of the Eve ('Eva'), indicating that the harm which came about through Eve is reversed through Mary.
- This Annunciation carol should be sung with vigour and lively rhythms, but at such a tempo that phrase endings are not snatched.
- Some of the circular phrases will need careful tuning, especially in verse 4, where it may be felt advisable to ease the tempo a little to give the words (and change in tonality) more space.
- Take care over the falling octave at the end of verse 4 – the lower note will need attention so that it is carefully placed and well-tuned.

### 29. O my dear heart

- This lovely cradle-song text by the Wedderburn brothers dates from c. 1567. Most spellings have been modernized. The word *spreit* (meaning *spirit*) should rhyme with *sweet*, and *gloir* (*glory*) with *more*. *Richt* is the Scottish form of *right*. The *i* is short, as in *bring*, and the *ch* should be pronounced as in *loch*.
- The music should move in gently flowing quavers, with a feeling of three in a bar, not one. Think in eight-bar phrases, but take a short breath at the half-way points (after 'sweet' in bar 8, and in the corresponding places in bars 16, 27 and 35); longer breaths should be taken in bars 12 and 31.
- Particular care is needed to ensure that the rising major sixth at the end of the first verse (bars 19-20) and the rising major third at the end of the second (bars 38-39) are in tune. Keeping the tone bright will help to prevent any flattening in pitch. The following exercise will be useful. It should be practised with and without accompaniment.

### 30. Quem pastores laudavere

*(1) To him whom shepherds praised, when told by the angels 'Be not afraid: he is born, the king of glory'; (2) to him to whom the Magi journeyed, to whom they brought gold, frankincense and myrrh, to the victorious Lion to whom they sincerely offered these gifts; (3) to Christ the king, begotten of God, given to us through Mary: let 'praise, honour and glory' resound most justly.*

- The Latin text consists of one long sentence strung out over three verses (an extra verse, often inserted between verses 2 and 3, is a later addition which ignores this scheme; it is not set here). The whole carol invites us to sing a resounding song to Christ of 'praise, honour and glory'.
- The melody line stretches over a wide vocal range; make sure that the tone is even, particularly in bars 7-8 and similar places.
- The music falls into two-bar phrases. Don't make these phrases too obvious, and decide how to phrase the piece, and where to breathe.
- Be careful not to snatch the last notes of phrases, particularly when the note is only a quaver (e.g., bar 6).
- Keep a bright tone in the soprano 2 (or alto) line and keep the thirds and sixths in tune.
- In the last verse, make sure that the soprano 1 line sounds like a descant and that the soprano 2 (or alto) line dominates.

### 31. Still, still, still

- A flowing minim beat will help singers achieve the gentle lilt needed here. There should be a feeling of onward movement through each phrase.
- Aim for a warm legato line, making sure that the quavers are never hurried. Project the contrasting moods of the three verses with attention to the dynamics and a sensitive 'colouring' of important words.
- The leaps in the bars 1 and 9 of each verse need to be sung cleanly and with even tone. Take particular care over the interval of the falling diminished fifth (beat 2 of bar 5, etc.); if the singers can think of this as a 'small' interval the C sharp will not flatten.

### 32. Ring out with jocund chime

- The metronome marking can be regarded as flexible and the speed should be adjusted to ensure that the words are clearly and crisply enunciated.
- Ensure the minim is always the beat and avoid any feeling of 4/4 especially in the central *meno mosso* section.
- A slightly detached style would best capture the spirit of the text.
- 'Christmas bells' is an alternative title for this piece.

### 33. Sweet baby sleep!

- Although quite slow, try to give a lilting effect by emphasising the strong beats in the bar.
- Try to achieve gentle, legato singing throughout. This will involve some practice, particularly on intervals such as 'Sleep' in bar 4. Keep the placing of the voice the same so that these larger intervals sound effortless and do not 'bump' at all.
- The unaccompanied sections at the ends of verses should not sound too distant, at least to begin with, but the final bars of the carol need to fade into nothingness.
- Make sure that there is a D natural in bar 12 and not a D sharp.

## 34. The darkest midnight in December

- The melody and accompaniment are written low in pitch, making this suitable for alto (or lower) voices to sing. The piece could be sung as an alto solo, or by unison voices. Bear in mind text and the title, and try to produce a dark tone, particularly at the start of verse 1.
- In the latter part of each verse, ensure that the G sharps and G naturals are observed properly (e.g., in bar 32 make sure that the rising triplet contains a G sharp, despite having heard a G natural in the previous bar.)
- Decide on the breathing points before singing this so that the flow of the melody and the meaning of the text are not interrupted.
- There are occasions where the melody line is at a dissonance with the accompaniment. This will need careful rehearsal to ensure that the vocal part sounds confident, smooth and effortless throughout.

## 35. Unfinished story

- The melody of this carol is fairly straight forward and 'catchy', but be careful to get the syncopated rhythms accurate – for example in bars 17-18 at the words 'unfinished story'. At bars 40-47 (and the corresponding phrase at bars 57-64) the rhythm in the lower part may need a little practice.
- Observe the dynamic markings (e.g., *mp* at bar 47) – dynamic variety helps keep the piece interesting for the listener.
- The 'rejoice' sections should be strong and joyful.
- For an alternative ending, some choirs may like to add harmony to the final note – perhaps a four-note chord:

## 36. The joyful sounds of salvation

- This carol needs energy but the tempo should not be rushed.
- Aim for clear consonants and if possible a rolled 'r' on 'rings'.
- Use the following exercise as a way of focusing on the correct style:

## 37. The rose-tree carol

- The author tells us: 'Since 1930 I have written a verse for my Christmas card.' This one was sent in 1949. The simplicity of this lovely text, with its reassuring ABAB rhyme scheme, is deceptive. Like so many fine Christmas carols it refers to the events of Good Friday. At such darker moments, chromatic notes appear, unsettling the comfortable world of consecutive thirds and orderly suspensions: careful tuning is needed.

- The time signature 6/8 may also be deceptive: neither plodding quavers nor a breezy two-in-a-bar is appropriate – aim for something in between: a thoughtful pace with a slight lilt.
- The mention of 'Blood' and 'Calvary' in the refrain provides the heart of the matter. This is not a cosy carol. But nothing should be over-stated; note *Semplice* at the beginning.
- The two quick syllables of 'flower' and 'bower' in verse 1 should be sung gently.

## 38. Waiting for the word
- The melody and accompaniment are written low in pitch, making this suitable for alto (or lower) voices to sing. The piece could be sung as a solo, or by unison voices.
- The melody should be kept flowing easily.
- Ensure that the syncopations are accurate but keep them as gentle as possible.
- To introduce some variety between the verses make sure that the dynamics are brought out. You could also alternate between solo and tutti verses.

## 39. Watts's cradle song
- Only five of Isaac Watts's fourteen stanzas (published in 1706) are used in this setting.
- The legato phrasing needs to be shaped with a gentle, lullaby lilt to the rhythm and care should be taken with tuning, especially of accidentals.
- Full musical advantage should be taken of the suspensions and their resolutions.
- Verse 3 should contrast in mood and colour with the other verses.
- Take care over the descant in bars 27 and 35 as it leaps up a third onto the seventh of a chord. This will be difficult to tune accurately and will need practice to make sure it is confident.

## 40. Welcome yule
- A few of the original fifteenth-century words have been given modern spellings and the second word of the title sounds better sung as 'yewl' rather than 'yool'.
- Make sure that the staggered entries from bars 22-26 are not late. In order to achieve this, each part will need to breathe in good time.
- Try to bring out the hemiola in bars 51-55.
- This work calls for rhythmic drive throughout with a one-in-a-bar pulse. Ensure the original speed is maintained in the quieter third stanza ('Candlemass') and avoid adding to the measured *rit* at the end of that passage.

## 41. What star is this?
- The opening time-signature of 7/8 should not phase anybody these days, but if you need to develop a sense of natural lilt, driven by rhythmic energy, use the following as a short clapping exercise (as confidence increases with repetition, try missing out syllables one at a time):

- If you do this exercise at the end of a practice, the week before the choir sees the music, they'll go home with that rhythm in their heads, and come back the following week ready to add the words and music…!
- In addition to a sense of natural lilt, the rhythm of this carol needs drive and clarity. This will be helped by crisp enunciation of the text.
- Once the singers are really confident with the tune of verse 1, the accompanist is at liberty to miss out the notes which double the vocal line, leaving just the accompanying chords.

- At various points, experienced singers may spot some oblique quotations to other carols: *How brightly shines*; *We three kings* and (more tenuously) *People, look East*. In each case, there's something in the words which links these carols together.
- In verse three, the change to 4/4 must not allow a relaxing of the pulse – go for a really smooth line but in strict time.
- The final verse sees a descant – purely to decorate, not dominate. In the first half of the verse, the descant part may come in late. Practise the descant only with the accompanying chords, perhaps with the chorus giving the spoken exercise (as above). At the third 'to God', the 'God' will need to be a fraction shorter than the other two, so that 'Three' is not late.
- The three 'Alleluias' have different syllable-rhythms – spoken practice with or without accompaniment may help to get them really clear.
- Resist the temptation to slow down at the end – choir and congregation should then experience a gasp of satisfaction after the last chord!

## 42. Zither carol

- This needs to be sung in a lively style. Suggested metronome mark: crotchet = 116.
- Pay particular attention to the enunciation of the words. They could, in fact, be spoken rather than sung in tempo and used as a diction exercise. When doing this maintain a loose jaw and employ the lips, teeth and tongue athletically.
- In each verse bars 4 and 5, 9 and 10, and 17 and 18 should be sung more smoothly than the rest of